# The Love Book

## Other books by the authors

52 Dates for You and Your Mate

The Ultimate Marriage Builder:
A Do-It-Yourself Encounter Weekend
for You and Your Mate

The Marriage Track

60 One-Minute Marriage Builders

# The Love Book

DAVE & CLAUDIA ARP

A JANET THOMA BOOK

THOMAS NELSON PUBLISHERS
Nashville • Atlanta • London • Vancouver

Published in Nashville, Tennessee, by Thomas
Nelson, Inc., Publishers, and distributed in Can-
ada by Word Communications, Ltd., Rich-
mond, British Columbia.

**Library of Congress
Cataloging-in-Publication Data**

Arp, Dave.
  The love book : over 300 ways to say
"I love you" / Dave & Claudia Arp.
    p.   cm.
  ISBN 0-7852-8017-0
  1. Love—Miscellanea.   I. Arp, Claudia.
II. Title.
HQ801.A76   1995
306.7—dc20                        94–34243
                                      CIP

Printed in Singapore
1 2 3 4 5 6 — 99 98 97 96 95 94

*To the participants in our*
*Marriage Alive Workshops*
*from Hong Kong to Budapest*
*and across the United States*
*who shared with us*
*what real love is!*

# Acknowledgments

Love is having supportive family and friends who shared their time, talent, and creativity with us in putting together this fun little book.

We especially acknowledge and thank Jeanne La-Borde Arp, Ken Coors, Laurie Clark, Amy Glass, Amy Clark, Janet Thoma, and the great in-house staff at Thomas Nelson.

# Love Is . . .

A favorite song from our dating days was "Love Is a Many-Splendored Thing." It described the energy, enthusiasm, and excitement of our growing love for each other.

Perhaps you also remembered the thrills of "young love," but over time things began to settle down. Did you, like us, discover that the person you thought was just about perfect also had some irritating habits? The stars in our eyes faded enough to see each other's idiosyncracies!

While love is still "a many splendored-thing," the reality of living together creates tension that can cloud the skies of romantic bliss. We all need reminders to love one another. That's why we put together this little book of ways to love each other just a little bit better.

Love is an attitude of caring more for the other person than caring for yourself. And love is expressed in little acts of kindness.

We challenge you to think about what love is to you. To get you started, here are 320 ways to complete the sentence "Love is . . ."

# Love Is . . .

*1*

Lying together on the grass
watching the clouds

*2*

Celebrating a gourmet picnic
in the park

*3*

Enduring frigid feet on your warm
legs on a cold winter night

*4*

Putting new shoe strings in his
old sneakers when you'd
prefer to throw them out

*5*

Picking wildflowers together

*6*

*Offering your warm jacket
to her when she is cold*

## 7
Skiing down blue slopes together
when you would rather be
on the black

## 8
Navigating the bedroom without
turning on the light

### 9
Going for a walk in the rain

### 10
Volunteering together
at a soup kitchen

### 11
Leaving confetti hearts in his
underwear when he's
leaving for a trip

Dave & Claudia Arp

**12**
Bringing him a cup of coffee in bed

**13**
Saying, "Don't worry, I'll do it,"
and actually doing it

**14**
Going shopping together when you'd
rather do anything else

*15*
Doing laundry together

*16*
Sharing your toothbrush

*17*
Paying the bills

Dave & Claudia Arp

**18**
Giving her a bird feeder

**19**
Refilling the bird feeder

**20**
Watching the birds together

*21*

*Putting lotion on his hands*
*after he does the dishes*

### 22
Exercising together after the holidays

### 23
Letting her read the mail first

### 24
Folding his towel and putting
it back on the rack

## 25
Going to the neighborhood drugstore
and buying the pregnancy test

## 26
Calling the plumber

*Dave & Claudia Arp*

*27*
Going to the ballet instead
of the Mets game

*28*
Going to the Mets game instead
of the ballet

32

*Putting flowers on the
doorstep, ringing the bell,
then running and hiding*

### 33
Toasting him and telling him why
you're glad you are married

### 34
Telling him he has spinach
between his front teeth

Dave & Claudia Arp

*38*
*Lighting a scented candle*
*in your bedroom*

*39*
Playing tennis without keeping score

*40*
Filling his car with gas

*41*
Canceling cable

### 42
Holding the ladder while
she cleans the gutters

### 43
Cleaning the gutters

### 44
Shoveling snow off the driveway

### 45
Supporting him when he is sure
his convictions are right

### 46
Just holding her when she
is sad or upset

### 47
Being silly together

### 48
Going fishing together

### 49
Baiting her fish hook

*50*

Sharing excitement over
each other's accomplishments

*51*

Truly listening to and
appreciating your in-laws

52

*Counting to ten
when you're angry*

### 53
Going for a walk in the snow

### 54
Lying together on a blanket
watching the stars

### 55
Saying thank you

*56*
Holding his coat
while shopping together

*57*
Always fastening your seat belt

*58*
Reminding her to fasten her seat belt

### 59
#### Cleaning out the garage

### 60
#### Cleaning out the attic

### 61
#### Putting a lock on the bedroom door

## 62

Mowing the grass
before it's a foot high

## 63

Leaving a midnight snack for your
night owl when you're a day lark

*64*

Surprising her with her favorite tea

*65*

Buying his favorite
perfume or cologne

*66*

Refilling her glass

67

*Building a fire
on a cold winter night*

*68*

Decorating the Christmas
tree together

*69*

Eating green M&Ms

*70*

Watching TV sports when
you really aren't into it

*71*

Checking the oil in her car

*72*

Not using the ATM card

*73*

Cleaning out the refrigerator

*74*

Refilling the sugar bowl

*75*

Watching each other's
favorite TV shows

*76*

Picking up your mother-in-law
at the airport

## 77

Slowing down and walking
at his pace

## 78

Speeding up and walking
at her pace

## 79

Writing thank you notes
for both of you

Dave & Claudia Arp

80
*Picking up sea shells together*

## 81
Watching the sun rise together

## 82
Sitting alone together
in the dark necking

## 83
Doing nothing together

*84*

Making up the bed when
you get up last

*85*

Hanging up his coat

*86*

Listening to the wind together

### 87
Cross-country skiing together

### 88
Daring each other to go
rock climbing

### 89
Sharing your feelings
when you're down

*90*
Listening while the other shares
his or her feelings

*91*
Asking, "What's the best thing that
happened to you today?"

*92*
Volunteering to put the Christmas
lights on the house

*93*
Delivering Christmas cookies
together to friends and neighbors

Dave & Claudia Arp

94
*Learning to sail together*

*95*
Replacing that light bulb

*96*
Bringing in the paper
when it's cold outside

*97*
Farming the kids out for an evening

## 98
Believing in each other

## 99
Saying, "Go for it. I know
you can do it!"

*100*

Holding hands when one of you is
discouraged and not saying,
"I told you so"

*101*

Sharing the best and worst
of your day

## 102
Writing out your commitment to
each other on your anniversary

## 103
Starting a new tradition

104
*Reading out loud together*

*105*
Going on a nature hike

*106*
Exploring new horizons together

*107*
Encouraging her to learn
something new

## 108
Holding the door open for each other

## 109
Holding hands

## 110
Holding on the phone when she
picks up the call waiting

111

*Laughing at yourself*

*112*
Making a scrapbook together

*113*
Putting a Valentine personal ad
in the newspaper

*114*
Being on time

*115*
Giving a hug

*116*
Leaving a note

*117*
Sending a plant or flowers

*118*
Taking out the trash

*119*
Calling him just to flirt

*120*
Washing his car

Dave & Claudia Arp

*121*
*Reading a love poem to her*

### 122
Making his favorite goodie

### 123
Trading back rubs

### 124
Making a tape of his favorite music

### 125
Renting a movie you know
he wants to see

### 126
Serving her breakfast in bed

### 127
Giving her a coupon for something
you know she wants to do

### 128
Taking her car to Jiffy Lube

### 129
Getting out of bed five minutes early
and putting on her favorite music

*130*
Cleaning out the walk-in closet
so you can walk in

*131*
Oiling that squeaky door

*132*
Serving a special meal on
china and crystal

### 133
Growing a special flower for him

### 134
Planting a tree on her birthday

### 135
Renting a billboard
for a special message

Dave & Claudia Arp

136
*Knowing when to be quiet*

## 137
Being the first to willingly
answer the phone

## 138
Checking out a book for him
at the library

## 139
Returning her overdue books
to the library

### 140
Polishing his shoes

### 141
Taking her shoes with the run down
heels to the shoe shop

### 142
Picking up her clothes

143
*Warming his side of the bed*
*on a cold evening*

### 144
Volunteering to stay home
when a child gets sick

### 145
Giving a donation to her favorite
charity in her honor

*146*

Learning to say, "We don't respond
to telephone solicitations"

*147*

Saying, "We don't respond to
telephone solicitations"

*Dave & Claudia Arp*

## 148
Offering to make an emergency trip
to the grocery store

## 149
Surprising him with a half gallon
of his favorite ice cream

*150*
*Breaking an irritating*
*or unhealthy habit*

### 151
Scraping off the ice
on her windshield

### 152
Warming up his car
when it's cold outside

### 153
Warming his nose on your cheek

154
Saying "I'm sorry" first

*155*

Framing a picture of the two of you

*156*

Getting up before him and turning
up the heat or lighting a fire

### 157
Letting her read her favorite section
of the paper first

### 158
Giving her romantic music

*159*

Throwing away those strange things
growing in the refrigerator

*160*

Making a list of things you love
about each other

### 161
Taking the initiative to call the doctor
when you both get the flu bug

### 162
Giving him two ice cubes
when there are only three

Dave & Claudia Arp

*163*
Telling her when she has lipstick
on her teeth

*164*
Sharing your breath mints

*165*
Giving her a head rub

*166*
Washing his hair

*167*
Rubbing noses

168
Making apple walnut
pancakes on Sunday
morning

*169*
Letting him have the last
piece of cake

*170*
Waiting to eat together when she is
late getting home—even though
you're hungry!

*Dave & Claudia Arp*

### 171
Cleaning up the puppy accident

### 172
Making the call no one
wants to make

### 173
Volunteering to return the calls
on the answering machine

### 174
Negotiating with the car mechanic

### 175
Giggling together

### 176
Buying chicken soup, crackers, and
Nyquil when the other is sick

Dave & Claudia Arp

*177*
*Retrieving the tennis ball*
*when she hits it over*
*the fence*

### 178
Rubbing sports cream
on his hurting back

### 179
Letting her choose the movie

### 180
Sharing a bag of popcorn

### 181
Being spontaneous

### 182
Cleaning the bathroom

*183*
Laughing at her jokes

*184*
Taking him home when he's yawning

*185*
Sharing a chocolate malt

186
Lingering in your favorite
restaurant over a cup
of cappuccino

### 187
Opening your home to her extended
family when you'd rather be alone

### 188
Getting the remote control after you
both are snuggled down in bed

*189*
Saying, "Go back to sleep honey,
I'll get the baby"

*190*
Scratching his itch in the middle
of the night

*191*
Leaving the last slice of pizza

*192*
*Giving her a foot massage*
*and lotion treatment*

Dave & Claudia Arp

### 193
Cleaning the tub for her when she's
too pregnant to bend over

### 194
Scrubbing the kitchen floor

*195*
Having a weekly alone time

*196*
Bringing him a silly gift
from a business trip

*197*
Fixing her favorite meal
even when you don't like it

### 198
Emptying the dishwasher

### 199
Taking the kids out for a few hours
to give her time to just be home alone

### 200
Going backpacking together

### 201
Kissing her when she
has coffee breath

### 202
Shaving on Saturday

### 203
Fixing breakfast for the kids
while she sleeps late

### 204
Giving her a Mother's Day card
from your new baby

### 205
Giving him a Father's Day card
from your new baby

### 206
Fixing his lunch

### 207
Getting up early to take the dog out

### 208
Making him a meal at 10 P.M.
when you have already eaten

Dave & Claudia Arp

209
*Praying together*

*The Love Book*

### 210
Laughing at his corny jokes

### 211
Not complaining about all the
unfinished projects around the house

### 212
Starting a tradition of dating
each other

### 213
Writing a love note on a napkin and
hiding it in her lunch

### 214
Holding on to each other when
the storm is raging outside

### 215
Putting toothpaste on his brush

### 216
Feeling threatened in a situation but
staying and participating for her sake

Dave & Claudia Arp

217
*Always kissing when
you say goodbye*

*218*
Dancing cheek to cheek

*219*
Forgiving each other

*220*
Flying a kite together

*221*
Writing "I love you" on her
frosted windshield

*222*
Whispering "I love you" in his ear

### 223

Turning your socks right side out
before throwing them into the
clothes hamper

### 224

Hitting the snooze button just once
when it's her day off

225
*Giving in when you still
believe you're right*

*226*

Getting out of bed to turn
off the last light

*227*

Forgoing mushrooms on the pizza
because he doesn't like them

228
*Not buying the car you
want because he read that it
did poorly in crash tests*

### 229
Listening to her talk late at night
when all you want to do is sleep

### 230
Dreaming the same dream

### 231
Taking a bath by candlelight

Dave & Claudia Arp

232
*Sleeping on one-third of a
queen size bed to keep warm*

### 233

Living in an area of town you would
rather not because the other needs
to be there due to school, work,
or family

### 234

Clipping the hair in his ear

### 235
Forgiving him when he leaves the
toilet seat up and you sit in the ice
cold bowl in the middle of the night

### 236
Coming home from work in time
to watch *Mystery* together

## 237
Being patient when she rolls over
and takes all the covers

## 238
Seeing your "special" child
complete a task

## 239
Giving her hours of back rubs
while she's in labor

240
Sensing the right time to
speak unspoken thoughts

### 241
Parking in the driveway so he can
use the garage to work on a project

### 242
Giving each other the chance
to go back to school

### 243

Turning off the light even though
you want to keep reading

### 244

Falling asleep with the light on so
your spouse can keep reading

### 245
Eating vegetarian because
he is vegetarian

### 246
Cooking meat for her even
though you're a vegetarian

### 247
Saying, "I love you" in the middle
of a busy intersection

Dave & Claudia Arp

### 248
Letting her tear the kitchen apart
to redecorate even though it
may take years to finish

### 249
Giving her a clean handkerchief
during a sad movie

250
Wanting to give an inch
but giving a mile

## 251
Mowing the lawn on a hot day so he
doesn't have to do it after work

## 252
Doing the dishes together

## 253
Listening with an open mind

*254*
Taking the kids to work for a day
(giving the stay-at-home spouse
a day off)

*255*
Letting him do it his way, even if you
don't think it's the right way

## 256
Listening to the same stories
for ten years and still laughing

## 257
Running a hot bubble bath for him
and watching the kids

258
Trusting each
other's faithfulness

259
Not minding when he decides
not to shave for a week

260
Snuggling under a blanket
on the couch

### 261
Eating meat loaf

### 262
Doing her chores

### 263
Admitting you still love him
after he shaved his head

## 264
Going out to fill a prescription
at 3 A.M.

## 265
Nursing him through a stomach virus

## 266
Ironing her blouse when she's
running late

267
Running your hand along
the massive dent and saying,
"Don't worry honey,
it's you I love,
not the car"

### 268
Giving him a hug when
he doesn't expect it

### 269
Not getting angry when she backs
through the garage door—for
the second time

*270*
Asking for directions
when you're lost

*271*
Getting out of bed and putting on
glasses to find that buzzing insect

### 272
Taking a class together

### 273
Cutting each other's hair

### 274
Moving to the couch instead
of waking the snoring spouse

### 275
Listening to jazz when you'd
really rather not

### 276
Making her favorite dessert

277
*A special smile across*
*a crowded room*

*278*
Getting ready early for an
important appointment

*279*
Letting your spouse use the
bathroom first when you
both need to go

## 280
Refilling the ice trays

## 281
Encouraging your spouse to relax
after work even though you feel
like asking for help

282

*Calling her during the day
just because you miss her
and want to hear her voice*

### 283
Eating an experimental meal and
offering a tactfully truthful opinion

### 284
Helping her turn over in bed when
she's nine months pregnant

### 285
Cleaning the lint screen in the dryer

### 286
Giving him an uninterrupted half day
to "work" on the computer

### 287
Going through labor and
childbirth together

### 288
Decorating the baby room together

### 289
Scratching the itch she can't reach

*290*
*Keeping your humor when*
*the wee ones have*
*exhausted you*

**291**

Taking the four pair of shoes from
the TV room back to the bedroom

**292**

Listening when you want to talk

293
*Letting her keep the kitten*

### 294
#### Kissing before you brush your teeth

### 295
#### Brushing your teeth before you kiss

### 296
#### Not nagging him to lose weight

## 297

Putting the car in the garage for the
night after he has taken off his shoes
and settled into a comfortable chair

## 298

Baby-sitting for her friend so
they can go out together

Dave & Claudia Arp

*299*
A big hug

*300*
A new baby

*301*
Skinny dipping

*302*
*Teaching your children to*
*respect you both*

### 303
Putting up the cows when
they get out

### 304
Listening to each other's
child-rearing advice

### 305
Buying her a turbo spa for
her tired muscles

*306*
Looking interested when he explains
how he fixed the . . .

*307*
Helping to rearrange the
furniture . . . again

### 308
Going without your favorite ice
cream and cookies so your wife
can lose her pregnancy weight

### 309
Laughing when you would rather cry

*310*
*Feeling free to show affection*
*for each other at any time*
*or any place*

## 311
Conceiving a child

## 312
Birthing a child

## 313
Training a child

## 314
Letting go of a child

*315*

Wearing the Santa Claus hat
at Christmas time

*316*

Leaving love notes in surprise
places (like in the sugar bowl or
underneath the toilet seat)

*317*
Putting the caps back on their
respective containers

*318*
Being protective when someone
hurts her

*319*
Making a special T-shirt with
hearts and *I love yous*

320
Thanking God for all the
years he has given
you together

If this little book inspires you to love each other in new and creative ways, we'd like to hear from you. You can write to us at:

Marriage Alive International
P.O. Box 90303
Knoxville, TN 37990

And if *The Love Book* encourages you to invest more time in your marriage, you'll find a fun guide for doing just that in our book *The Ultimate Marriage Builder*.

Blessings!